Unity is Peace

An address by
SRI MATA AMRITANANDAMAYI DEVI

Translated by
Swami Amritaswarupananda

at the INTERFAITH CELEBRATION in honor of
the 50th ANNIVERSARY OF THE UNITED NATIONS
NEW YORK, OCTOBER 21, 1995

Uɴɪᴛʏ ɪs Pᴇᴀᴄᴇ
An address by SRI MATA AMRITANANDAMAYI DEVI
at the INTERFAITH CELEBRATION in honor of
the 50th Anniversary of the United Nations, October 21, 1995.

Translated by
Swami Amritaswarupananda

Published by
Mata Amritanandamayi Mission Trust
Amritapuri, Kollam 690 525
Website: www.amritapuri.org
Email: info@theammashop.org

| *First eight editions:* | 1996-2011 | 24.000 copies |
| *Ninth edition* | 2013 | 1.000 copies |

Typesetting and Layout
  Amrita D.T.P., Amritapuri

Copyright © 1995 by Mata Amritanandamayi Mission Trust

All rights reserved. No part of this publication may be stored in a
retrieval system, transmitted, reproduced, transcribed or translated into
any language, in any form, by any means without the prior agreement
and written permission of the publisher.

Contents

Preface	4
Introduction	7
Unity is Peace	13
The complete version of Amma's address	28

Preface

Can you imagine an ordinary village girl from a remote fishing village in southern India, who never completed her formal education, who is utterly humble and earthy in appearance, clad in simple white clothes, speaking at the Parliament of the World's Religions in Chicago, in September 1993, a platform shared by many eminent scholars from all over the world; and later delivering a speech at the Interfaith Celebration which was held in New York, in honor of the fiftieth anniversary of the UN, and there capturing the attention and the appreciation of the most learned people? Living in an age in which the existence of God and the relevance of spirituality is being seriously questioned and even criticized, what explanations can the so-called intellectuals and skeptics give to such an irresistible personality as Amma, the Divine Mother Amritanandamayi Devi?

Our modern society, in which people are running frantically after the passing fancies of life, has become overwhelmed by disappointments and frustrations. Science is taking big leaps forward, but at the same time, the existence of human beings on the face of the earth is being confronted with

several serious threats. Mankind has lost touch with real life, which is based on higher values. This age, which can truly be called "the Age of Agony," needs a spiritual solution to awaken human beings from their sleep. It is high time that we take a good look at the problems that beset each country, and that we try to solve those problems from a spiritual angle. As Mother rightly says in Her speech, "Science, which so far has developed through the human intellect, can only be perfected through meditation. Only through the knowledge of the inner Self can science reach its highest peak."

Speaking on "Visions for the 21st Century," Mother, in Her own simple and lucid way, talks about the basic problems of life and suggests spiritual solutions.

Only great Masters like Mother, who have dived deep into their own consciousness, can guide humanity along the right path. True national integration and unity between different countries and their people can only take place in the Light and Love that the Masters sow in the hearts of human beings. The radiant presence of a true Master is the most fertile soil from where we can simply slip out into the light of real freedom, love, and unity, like buds nourished in the earth slipping out into the warm spring sun.

50th Anniversary of the United Nations

Only through love can humanity be united. As Amma mentions in Her speech, "A drop of water cannot be a river; a river is formed by numerous water drops. It is the joining together of countless drops that creates a flow. The real flow of life lies in unity, in the oneness that arises out of love."

The phenomenon known as Mata Amritanandamayi is as mysterious as the universe. The closer we are to Her the more mysterious She becomes. I don't know how you, the reader, would explain the wondrous phenomenon that Mother is. A person like myself can only bow down in utter silence, humility, and surrender in front of this incredible and incomprehensible personality, who, I believe, is Sarvatita, who is beyond everything—the very Principle of the Beyond.

The words that are contained in this book will give the reader a glimpse of the infinite wisdom that Mother imparts to the human race.

Swami Amritaswarupananda

Introduction

A wave of whispers, "Who is She? . . ." "Who is that? . . ." "Who. . .?" "Who. . .?" "Who. . .?" filled Synod Hall at the Cathedral of Saint John the Divine in New York as numerous cameras flashed and necks craned to watch as our beloved Amma entered to take Her seat. The occasion was the recent gathering of religious leaders in celebration of the 50th Anniversary of the United Nations on October 21. It was no reflection on the speaker who happened to be at the podium when heads turned away from him 180 degrees towards the Shining Light who has stolen all our attention and our hearts. After all, no one could successfully vie for the attention of more than a fifth of the attendees who seemed to be fervent devotees of Amma representing satsang groups in every region of the US, Canada and more.

Amma was actively pursued as a special guest speaker by the organizing committee for the UN Conference on "Visions for the 21st Century." As usual, She kept everyone guessing about Her participation until the last minute when hundreds of devotees rushed to the airlines and ticket agencies to arrange their journey to meet Amma in New York.

Amma's main UN presentation was on Saturday, October 21. She shared a panel in the afternoon with Nobel Peace Prize winner, Oscar Arias, ex-President of Costa Rica and Dada Vaswani, head of the Sadhu Vaswani Mission.

Later that evening, Amma, Swami Amritaswarupananda, Swami Ramakrishnananda, Swami Amritatmananda, Swami Premananda, Swamini Amrita Prana, Swamini Krishnamrita Prana and Br. Dayamrita Chaitanya all walked together in a procession with other religious leaders inside the cathedral. Each tradition presented a prayer, a song or a dance in celebration of the divine unity of all.

There was a valedictory peace invocation led by the spiritual leaders representing each religion, and Amma, representing the Sanatana Dharma, chanted the mantra, "Om Lokah Samastah Sukhino Bhavantu," as everyone joined in.

The UN anniversary began with prayers and visions from the ancient religious traditions of the world, for true compassion can only be attained through spiritual practices. In Awaken Children, volume 5, Amma says that compassion is an extension of faith in the existence of all-pervading Love. "When love becomes Divine Love, compassion also fills the heart. Love is the inner feeling and compassion is its expression. Compassion does not see the faults of others. It does not see the weaknesses of people. It makes no distinction between good and bad people. Compassion cannot draw a line between two countries, two faiths or two religions. Compassion has no ego; thus there is no fear, lust or passion. Compassion simply forgives and forgets. Compassion is like a passage. Everything passes through it. Nothing can stay there. Compassion is love expressed in all its fullness."

The Temple of Understanding and the Council of Religious and Interfaith Organizations sponsored this conference, a forum for religious leaders, diplomats, NGO's, and educators to present their visions for the next century. A conference statement was to be presented to the UN while the 50th Anniversary Summit was still in session. Dr. Karan Singh, the Chair of the Temple of Understanding, opened the session with sacred verses. He elaborated on the intention of the celebration which was inspired by the acknowledgment of the need for the "political dimensions to be informed by the spiritual dimensions," that the UN and UNESCO must provide a new paradigm of thought which centers on the responsibility for fostering global values of caring, compassion and tolerance. The thirty-two speakers included religious leaders from various traditions as well as a few heads of state and scholars. Other religions represented were Buddhism, Christianity, Judaism, Islam, Shintoism, Sikhism, Zoroastrianism, Baha 'I, and Akuapim Traditional Religion of Ghana.

The interfaith assembly called for interactive support of the religious community with the United Nations, UN Member States, and NGO's (non-governmental organizations). Jonathan Granoff, Chairman of the Conference, writes, "The dominant institutional framework in the world today is the nation-state. The stability of nations is the dominant institutional framework out of which United Nations' activities originate. We propose an added dimension: the expression of full humanity based on universal values with social theory and social policy manifesting these values. This fundamentally moral foundation for social policy can no longer be ignored. We can enliven the heart and vision of humanity only if we tap its deeper roots. The world needs nothing less."

Amma's entrance into the Hall and Her presence during the presentations was dazzling, and Her unique message, interpreted by Swami Amritaswarupananda, was refreshing to ears yearning to hear the Truth which only a Mahatma can give.

Unity is Peace

An address by
SRI MATA AMRITANANDAMAYI DEVI

Translated by
Swami Amritaswarupananda

at the INTERFAITH CELEBRATION in honor of
the 50th ANNIVERSARY OF THE
UNITED NATIONS
NEW YORK, OCTOBER 21, 1995

Unity is Peace

An address by Holy Mother Amritanandamayi Devi at the Cathedral of St. John The Divine, New York, on the occasion of the fiftieth anniversary of the United Nations, October 21, 1995.

Salutations to all those present, who are verily of the nature of Supreme Love.

Mother would like to take this opportunity to express her appreciation for the dedicated efforts of those serving the United Nations and the Temple of Understanding in the interest of world peace. May their work find growing support amongst the people and nations of the world.

To grow and develop is the slogan of all nations and individuals in the modern age. Isn't it good to grow and develop? Certainly! Those are the signs of real life. Life itself would wither away if there were no growth and development. Without these two factors, life has no meaning. Many countries have experienced amazing economic growth. Nevertheless, there remain unending problems within these countries. There may exist external threats from other countries as well. In general, people in every country are

unsatisfied and restless, their minds are filled with fear and suspicion. The world is burning like a volcano; people and nations are ready to trample and destroy each other if given the opportunity.

Mother is not saying that goodness and good people have completely disappeared from the face of the earth. There are, of course, virtuous people and organisations like the United Nations, that are striving hard to restore the lost peace and harmony of this planet. But the goodness in the world is not growing at a pace to withstand the rapidly growing forces of evil. We have forgotten the love, concern, and trust that human beings are supposed to show each other. "As long as I get what I want, I don't care how it's done!" This is how many people think, and the thoughts of each individual are reflected and become part of the collective thoughts of a nation.

Life has almost become a battlefield, where there are no near and dear ones, but only enemies. Those fighting side by side today, later become divided and can be found fighting each other. The ego and selfishness of man has turned human relationships into a cheap businesslike

endeavour. Our concern for our fellow beings has been lost. Our qualities as real human beings are being sacrificed.

Many countries claim that they have made great progress in many fields. This may be true, but as a whole, their growth is stunted. A country may be growing externally, but the inner soul is becoming weaker.

A person is very handsome and has an attractive personality. But what if he is actually gravely ill? What if this same man happens to be dying of heart disease? This is the condition of many countries: the outer facade is greatly embellished, but the inside is falling apart.

There was a time when human beings would gaze at natural phenomena in utter wonderment. As time went on, they began observing and inquiring deeper into these phenomena, rather than simply watching them. Now, in this age of science, man is striving hard to dive deep into the mysteries of the universe. Science and the intellect has reached its peak. Yet there is one thing that remains unknown, beyond man's reach, and that is the infinite power of the inner Self. Man remains ignorant of the truth that the Universal Power exists within himself. This belief has not yet taken root in him. The supreme Truth can only be known through faith and meditation. Science, which so far has developed through the human intellect, can only be perfected through meditation. Only through the knowledge of the inner Self can science reach its highest peak.

Let our effort to discover our own essential nature—that indwelling Universal Power—be a characteristic feature of the new millennium we are about to enter. Let this be recognised as one of the important goals of the next century. We have nothing to lose by trusting the infinite power of the Self, except the bondage of our own ignorance. The chain of limitations that binds us must break, in order to open our hearts, to know each other, and to understand the pain and suffering of others by putting ourselves in their place.

As far as modern science is concerned, the entire world falls into two categories: the known and the unknown. In the future scientists may discover much of what is not yet known. But it is the unknowable, that which is far beyond the intellect, that we must seek to discover, and that is God, or our own true Self.

We may deny God, but the intellect cannot prove or disprove God. If the intellect were able to prove God's existence—if the intellect could contain God within its grasp—it would only mean that the intellect is greater than God. If God could be understood through the intellect, then God and religion wouldn't be necessary at all. Science and the intellect would be enough. A god under the control of the intellect is not what we need. What we need is faith in a Supreme Power that controls the entire universe, that is beyond the mind and senses, and which makes even the intellect function. We should enquire into the very Source of that Power, which exists within ourselves. Faith in that Cosmic Power, together with meditation to know that Supreme Power, alone will help us attain knowledge of the Self, unity, peace, and tranquillity.

That Power is the very substratum of our existence—and our existence cannot be denied. The truth "I exist" is self-evident. You may deny God by saying, "God is just a belief," but existence cannot be refuted. That existence, that Cosmic

UNITY IS PEACE

Power, is God. God has no separate hands, legs, eyes, or body, other than our own. He moves through our hands, He walks with our legs, He sees through our eyes, and it is He who beats within the heart of each one of us.

This universe is one, not many. Man has divided the world into fragments, not God. It is man, who, through his thoughts and actions, creates turmoil and disintegration in the natural, harmonious unity of the world. Each atom serves as a building block of this universe and is intrinsically connected to every other atom. This planet where we live is not an isolated entity functioning separately from the universe. Everything is part of the Whole. When something good and elevating happens somewhere, those vibrations are reflected in the one Universal Mind. In the case of an evil act, negative vibrations will be reflected. The intensity of the reflection depends on the intensity of the good and bad actions we perform. Unfortunately, in the modern world, human selfishness and evil have become predominant. As a result, the vibrations of the one world family reflects that negativity.

The people dwelling on this planet are the life of this world. We should show the same eagerness to create harmony in the inner world, as we show towards material progress in the external world. The thoughts and actions of the people give each country its power, vitality, and its peace.

In the past, nature protected, nourished, and sustained us. But, man's unintelligent interference and selfish exploitation of Mother Nature has upset her delicate balance. This is manifesting in negative effects throughout the world. The rain, wind, and sunshine, which used to come in proper proportion and season, now come irregularly, often with devastating effects. It is our responsibility to restore the lost harmony of nature.

People, especially the younger generation, are becoming addicted to drugs and other intoxicants, thus losing their vitality, creativity, and capacity to benefit themselves and the world. The younger generation, which is meant to blossom and give fragrance to the world, is instead withering away in the bud stage. One generation has already strayed from the path of righteousness. In

order to rebuild a healthy and wholesome society, the children must be taught moral and spiritual values. This emphasis should be integrated into the world's educational systems.

Redressing these crucial conditions, which affect the future of the world, should be recognised as an important goal of the 21st century.

The life force that pulsates in the trees, plants, and animals is the same life force that pulsates within us. The same life energy that gives us the power to speak and to sing, is the power behind the song of the bird and the roar of the lion. The same consciousness that flows in and through every human being, lends its power to the movement of the wind, to the flow of the river, and to the light of the sun. How can there be any sense of difference once this subtle principle is understood? When we evaluate our growth and development in the light of this great Truth, we may wonder whether we human beings have really developed or grown at all. The progress that we see today is divided growth. Only some parts are growing—the world as a whole remains unhealthy. We cannot call this real progress.

Let us take the human body as an example. The body as a whole, with all its internal and external organs, must grow in proper proportion to maintain its health and well-being. If the head alone grows, while other parts of the body remain undeveloped, such a person would become deformed and unhealthy.

The same principle applies to the world. Like the body, the world is a whole, a unity. The different nations are its different organs. Yet, today every country is concerned only with its own progress. The traditions and feelings of other nations and their people are completely ignored. If each nation is an organ, a part of the one world body, how can the growth of just one country be considered whole and integrated growth?

Human beings categorise and compartmentalise all areas of life. These divisions in the minds of individuals can cause division in the family, which in turn will be reflected in the society, in the nation, and in the whole world. This attitude of division is spreading like a contagious disease. The entire human race is being divided.

Unity is Peace

People are becoming divided both internally and externally. It is a far cry from unity and integration. The reason for this division and confusion is our ignorance of the essential principle of life.

One and the same rhythm and tune pulsates within all of creation. Once we realise this truth, all the contradictions and differences will dissolve and disappear. Then we will hear the eternal music of the Self, both within and without. The divine flower of peace, love, and tranquillity will blossom, and its fragrance will spread all over the world.

We have forgotten that working for the restoration of peace and unity in this world is the first and foremost duty of all human beings. To fulfill this duty, we must grow spiritually along with our material progress. Each nation should develop an attitude of oneness, giving up feelings of division. Each country should take steps towards material prosperity by planting its feet firmly on that foundation of oneness.

Each country should make a conscious effort to be more sensitive towards other nations. We should see each nation as an integral part of every other nation. Only when we make the

effort to understand the difficulties and the pain of other countries, can we act and work together in the unitary spirit of love. Only then will this world grow perfectly, as a unity, as a whole. Such growth alone will bring equanimity, brotherhood, and peace. Otherwise, the result is weakness and deterioration. No real growth will occur.

This world is like a flower. Each nation is a petal. If one petal is infested, does it not affect all the other petals? Does not the disease destroy the life and beauty of the flower? Is it not the duty of each one of us to protect and preserve the beauty and fragrance of this one world flower from being destroyed? This world of ours is a big, wonderful flower with many petals. Only when this is understood and becomes deeply ingrained in us, will there be any real peace and unity. The tug of war between nations is like a tug of war between the petals of a flower. Competition between the petals will only result in all the petals withering away. The entire flower will be destroyed. Division will only dissipate our energy and vitality; real power is to be found in unity, not in division.

The entire world will become our family once we realise our oneness with that Universal Power. Once this knowledge dawns in us, we can no longer work for just a few people, or for a single community, or for one particular nation. Once we realise this truth, the entire universe becomes our own abode. All of creation becomes our own. We behold that everything is pervaded with God-consciousness, with the Supreme Divine Power. Everything is seen as different names and forms of that Divine Power. This universe becomes our own body; the different nations and its people become parts of our universal body. People who experience this are beyond any division. They become totally undivided and integrated personalities. Such personalities are the embodiments of pure, untainted Love. Expressing that Divine Love through all their words and deeds, they inspire people and transform their lives.

Together we are a power, an undefeatable power. When we work together, hand in hand, with love, it is not just one life force but the

life energy of countless people, of the group, that flows in harmony, unimpeded. From that constant stream of unity, real progress will take place, and we will see the birth of peace.

A drop of water cannot be a river; a river is formed by numerous water drops. It is the joining together of countless drops that creates a flow. The real flow of life lies in unity, in the oneness that arises out of love.

Let us pray and meditate together. That is the way to reach the shore of peace. When we meditate and pray as a group, the life energy of all of us will harmoniously flow to a single stream spreading a divine fragrance soaked in the sweetness of love. This will create vibrations of peace and unity in the atmosphere. Attuning our minds with the one Supreme Power and forgetting all thoughts of division, let us open our hearts and sincerely utter the following prayer:

LOKAH SAMASTAH SUKHINO BHAVANTU
Let all beings in all the worlds be happy.

During such moments of prayer, the vibrations of the prayer will reflect in the minds of everyone, thus giving peace and tranquillity.

Om Shanti Shanti Shanti.

Peace Peace Peace.

50th Anniversary of the United Nations

UNITY IS PEACE

(The complete version of Amma's address)

To grow and develop is the slogan of all nations and individuals in the modern age. Isn't it good to grow and develop? Certainly! Those are the signs of real life. Life itself would wither away if there were no growth and development. Without these two factors, life has no meaning. Many countries have experienced amazing economic growth. Nevertheless, there remain unending problems within these countries. There may exist external threats from other countries as well. In general, people in every country are unsatisfied and restless. Their minds are full of fear and suspicion. The world is burning like a volcano. We are living in a world where people and nations are ready to trample and destroy each other if given the opportunity.

Mother is not saying that goodness and good people have completely disappeared from the face of the earth. There are, of course, virtuous people and organizations like the United Nations, that are striving hard to restore the lost peace and harmony of this planet. But the goodness in the world is not growing at a pace to withstand the rapidly growing forces of evil. We have forgotten the love, concern, and trust that human beings are supposed to show each other. "As long as I get what I want, I don't care how it's done!" This is how many people think, and the thoughts of each individual are reflected and become part of the collective thoughts of a nation. The material development of a country is not the only criterion by which the growth of a nation can be measured. Progress should also be evaluated in the light of the inherent tendencies of the people and the quality of their thoughts. Competing with each other for petty reasons, human beings are sacrificing the higher values of life. This is the condition of modern society. It is a tragic situation.

Life has almost become a battlefield. Relatives and friends, those once near and dear, often become enemies eagerly awaiting the opportunity of destroy each other. Those fighting together side by side today, later become divided and can be found fighting each other. Nowadays, this is a common sight in the world. The ego and

selfishness of man has turned human relationships into a cheap businesslike endeavor. Our concern for our fellow beings has been lost. Our qualities as real human beings are being sacrificed.

There is a story about a man who was involved in a lawsuit. He thought he might lose the case, and desperately told his lawyer that he was about to send the judge an entire set of golf clubs as a bribe. The lawyer was shocked and said to his client, "The judge takes great pride in his honesty. He cannot be bribed; if you do that, it will only serve to turn him against you."

The man won the case, and when it was all over, he invited his lawyer for dinner. He expressed his gratitude to the lawyer for his advice concerning the golf clubs. "I did, in fact, send them to the judge," he said, "but I sent them on behalf of our opponent."

This is how many people's minds work in the present day world. There is a lack of spiritual and human values.

Countries claim that they have made great progress in many fields. This may be true, but as a whole, their growth is stunted. A country may be growing externally, but the inner soul is becoming weaker.

A person is very handsome and has an attractive personality. Nobody can pass him by without glancing at him at least once. But what if he is actually gravely ill? What if this same man happens to be dying of heart disease? This is the condition of many countries: the outer facade is greatly embellished, but the inside is falling apart. Does this mean, then, that we are erring from the right path?

There was a time when man's intellect was less developed than it is today, when he beheld natural phenomena such as the ocean, a storm, thunder and lightning in utter wonderment. As time went on, as man's power of thinking deepened, he began observing and inquiring deeper into these phenomena, rather than simply watching them. He strove hard to dive deep into the mysteries of the universe. He invented many things through his experiments. He even discovered the ultimate components of the atom. He went to the moon. Many dreams, once considered to be unattainable, have now been achieved and are under his control. By man's sheer capacity of intellect, he has even established his supremacy in space. He has also developed computers to do almost any type of work. Yet, there is one thing that remains unknown, and beyond man's reach. That is the infinite power of his own Self. Man remains ignorant of the truth that the Universal Power exists within himself. This belief has not yet taken root in him. The supreme Truth can be attained only through faith and meditation.

Let our effort to discover our own essential nature—that indwelling Universal Power—be a characteristic feature of the new millennium we are about to enter. Let this be recognized as one of the important goals of the next century. We have nothing to lose by trusting the infinite power of the Self, except the bondage of our own ignorance. The chain of limitations that binds us must break, in order to open our hearts, to know each other, and to understand the pain

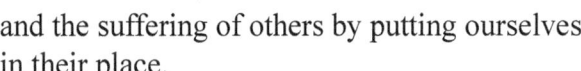

and the suffering of others by putting ourselves in their place.

Science, which so far has developed through the human intellect, can only be perfected through meditation. Only through the knowledge of the inner Self can science reach its highest peak. As far as modern science is concerned, the entire world falls into two categories: the known and the unknown. In the future scientists will discover much of what is not yet known. But it is the unknowable, that which is far beyond the intellect, that we must seek to discover. That is God, or our own Self.

We have the tendency to feel proud of our knowledge. But if we stop for a moment and think about it, we will realise that we are leading an almost unconscious life. How many times a day are we really aware of our own body? When we eat, we are neither aware of our own hand that feeds us, nor of the tongue in our mouth. When we walk, we are unaware of our own legs. Are we conscious of our breathing? As we look around and observe all the beauty and ugliness before us, are we aware of our own eyes? We are leading

an unconscious life. How can we feel proud and think that we are conscious and all-knowing?

We may deny God, but the intellect cannot prove or disprove God. If the intellect were able to prove God's existence—if the intellect could contain God within its grasp—it would only mean that the intellect is greater than God. If God could be understood through the intellect, then God and religion wouldn't be necessary at all. Science and the intellect would be enough. A god under the control of the intellect is not what we need. What we need is faith in a Supreme Power that controls the entire universe, that is beyond the mind and senses. Faith in that Cosmic Power, together with meditation to know that Supreme Power, alone will help us attain knowledge of the Self, unity, peace, and harmony.

We should enquire into the very Source of that power, which makes even the intellect function. That Power exists within ourselves. It is the very substratum of our existence—and our existence cannot be denied. The existence of the world, the existence of everything in nature, cannot be denied. The truth "I exist" is self-evident. You may deny God by saying, "God is just a

belief," but existence cannot be refuted. That existence, that Cosmic Power, is God. God has no separate hands, legs, eyes, or body, other than our own. He moves through our hands, He walks with our legs, He sees through our eyes, and it is He who beats within the heart of each one of us.

In a village there was a beautiful statue of a great Mahatma with its arms outstretched. On a plaque beneath the statue these words were inscribed: "Come into My arms!" One day a terrible riot took place in the village, there was a lot of destruction everywhere, and the statue was damaged—the arms were broken off. The villagers loved the statue and were very upset about the damage. They gathered together and decided to make new arms for the statue. But an old man stood up among them and said, "No, don't worry about making new arms for the statue. Let him be without arms."

The villagers wondered, "But what about the plaque underneath? It says, 'Come into my *arms*!'" The old man replied, "That is no problem. Just below the words, 'Come into my arms,' you should add, 'But I have no other arms than yours.'"

"Come into my arms, *but I have no other arms than yours*,"—that is what God is constantly telling us.

When a child is born, he or she is not conditioned by anything. But the people who surround the child—his parents, siblings, friends and society—teach him to acquire different habits. They raise him in a certain way, in a certain culture, with its own language, food, education, religion, customs, and habits. Everything around him conditions him. We teach him everything—except about the infinite power of his own Self.

Only human beings are self-conscious. A cow or a dog is not self-conscious. A cow never thinks, "I am an Indian cow or an American cow, a white or black cow, or a Jersey cow." Man alone is conscious of such differences.

This universe is one, not many. Man has divided the world into fragments, not God. It is man, who, through his thoughts and actions, creates turmoil and disintegration in the natural, harmonious unity of the world. Each atom serves as a building block of this universe and is intrinsically connected to every other atom. This planet where we live is not an isolated entity functioning separately from the universe. Everything is part of the Whole. When something good and elevating happens somewhere, those vibrations are reflected in the one Universal Mind. In the case of an evil act, negative vibrations will be reflected. The intensity of the reflection depends on the intensity of the good and bad actions we perform. Unfortunately, in the modern world, human selfishness and evil have become predominant. As a result, the vibrations of the one world family reflects that negativity.

The life force that pulsates in the trees, plants, and animals is the same life force that pulsates within us. The same life energy that gives us the power to speak and to sing, is the power behind the song of the bird and the roar of the lion. The same consciousness that flows in and through every human being, lends its power to the movement of the wind, to the flow of the river, and to the light of the sun. How can there be any sense of difference once this subtle principle is understood? When we evaluate our growth and development in the light of this great Truth, we may wonder whether we human beings have really developed or grown at all. The progress that we see today is divided growth. Only some parts are growing—the world as a whole remains unhealthy. We cannot call this real progress.

Let us take the human body as an example. The body as a whole, with all its internal and external organs, must grow in proportion to maintain its health and well-being. Only then can we consider it to be real growth. If the head alone grows, and all the other parts of the body remain undeveloped, it can only be considered as unhealthy, disproportionate growth. Such a person would become deformed and unhealthy. Similarly, nations must grow not only materially, but in spiritual and human values as well.

This is like the person who suffered from two ailments. His eyes troubled him and he had digestive problems. The man went to a doctor, who gave him eye drops and medicine for his stomach. Unfortunately, in his excitement, the patient confused the doctor's instructions; he went home and drank a dose of the eye drops and poured the stomach medicine into his eyes.

As a result, both his problems became more aggravated. Likewise, we are mixing up the two containers, taking the wrong medicine for the wrong ailment. There is great confusion today with regard to our lives. The importance that we presently give to the body and the external world should be directed towards developing our knowledge of the Universal Power dwelling within us. But we do it the other way around. The result is a world rapidly deteriorating.

The human mind is becoming more and more divided. There was a time when only one doctor was enough for all the different diseases. Today, we have doctors for every single disease. There is a doctor for the large intestine and a different doctor for the small intestine. The ear, nose, and throat specialist doesn't know much about the eyes, nor does the heart specialist know much about the stomach. They aren't interested in any parts other than their own field of specialisation. Only if the treatment considers the entire body as a whole, will the treatment be most effective. Then only can one attain perfect health.

How many doctors know everything about the entire body system? The doctors have

studied, but their knowledge remains only theoretical. In practical life they are only interested in one particular aspect of the body. Amma is not saying that specialisation is useless. Of course, it is beneficial; it has helped to determine the root cause of each disease and to develop effective treatment. Yet, from one doctor for the entire body, we have now reached a situation where we need one doctor for each organ of the body. The mind keeps on dividing. Human talents and capacities are not being tapped properly. Because of the divisions of the mind and our energies, our real talents are not being expressed. Due to this division, our power of concentration and vitality is weakening.

Human beings categorize and compartmentalize all areas of life. They divide everything. As the mind becomes divided, man's life also becomes divided. A division in the mind of an individual can cause division in the family, which in turn will be reflected in the society, in the nation, and in the whole world. This attitude of division is spreading like a contagious disease. The entire human race is being divided. People are becoming divided both internally and externally. It is a far cry from unity and integration. The reason for this division and confusion is our ignorance of the essential principle of life.

Like the body, this world is one whole—a unity. The different nations are its different organs. The people dwelling on this planet are the soul, the life, of this world. We should show the same eagerness to create harmony in the inner world—the very life of a country—as we show towards material progress in the external world. The thoughts and actions of the people give each country its power, vitality, and its peace.

In the past, nature protected, nourished, and sustained us. But man's unintelligent interference and selfish exploitation of Mother Nature has upset her delicate balance. This is manifesting in negative effects throughout the world. The rain, wind, and sunshine, which used to come in proper proportions and season, now come irregularly, often with devastating effects. It is our responsibility to restore the lost harmony of nature.

People, especially the younger generation, are becoming addicted to drugs and other intoxicants, thus losing their vitality, creativity, and capacity to benefit themselves and the world. The younger generation, which is meant to blossom and give fragrance to the world, is instead withering away in the bud stage. One generation has already strayed from the path of righteousness. In order to rebuild a healthy and wholesome society, the children must be taught moral and spiritual values. This emphasis should be integrated into the world's educational systems.

Redressing these crucial conditions, which affect the future of the world, should be recognized as an important goal of the 21st century.

One and the same rhythm and tune pulsates within all of creation. Once we realise this truth, all the contradictions and differences will dissolve and disappear. Then we will hear the eternal music of the Self, both within and without. The divine flower of peace and tranquillity will blossom, and its fragrance will spread all over the world.

Today every country is concerned only with its own progress. The feelings of others and

the traditions of other nations are completely ignored. When we evaluate this situation, considering the entire world as one single body, a unity, such growth can only be seen as partial growth. One nation is only an organ, a part of the one world body. How, then, can the so-called growth of just one country be considered whole and integrated growth? Such growth will never help us gain peace and unity, because the development of the other parts of the world body remain stunted.

People in many countries are suffering; people are being tortured. When a country makes no effort to understand and imbibe the feelings and traditions of another nation, or when it tries to trample that nation, it is like injuring our left hand with our right hand, or as if we were trying to poke out our own eye. It is like a person torturing the members of his own family just for the sake of fulfilling his desires.

We have forgotten that working for the restoration of peace and unity in this world is the first and foremost duty of all human beings. Without realising the underlying oneness of the Self—the one, all-pervading Consciousness—peace and unity cannot be attained. To fulfill this duty, we must grow spiritually along with our material progress. Each nation should develop an attitude of oneness, of unity, giving up feelings of division. Each country should take steps towards material prosperity by planting its feet firmly on that foundation of oneness.

Each country should make a conscious effort to understand others and to be more sensitive towards other nations. We should see each nation as an integral part of every other nation. Only when we make the effort to understand the difficulties and the pain of other countries, can we act and work together in the unitary spirit of love. Only then will this world grow perfectly, as a unity, as a whole. Such growth alone will bring equanimity, brotherhood, and peace. Otherwise, the result is weakness and deterioration. No real growth will occur.

This world is like a flower. Each nation is a petal. If one petal is infested, does it not affect all the other petals? Does not the disease destroy the life and beauty of the flower? Is it not the duty of each one of us to protect and preserve the beauty and fragrance of this one world flower from being destroyed? This world of ours is a big, wonderful flower with many petals. Only when this is understood and becomes deeply ingrained within us, will there be any real peace and unity. The tug of war between nations is like a tug of war between the petals of a flower. Competition between the petals will only result in all the petals withering away. The entire flower will be destroyed. Division will only dissipate our energy and vitality; real power is to be found in unity, not in division.

The entire world will become our family once we realise our oneness with that Universal Power. Once this knowledge dawns in us, from then on, we cannot work for just a few people, or for a single community, or for one particular nation. Once we realize this truth, the entire universe becomes our own abode. All of creation becomes our own. We behold that everything is pervaded with God-consciousness, with Supreme Divine Power. Everything is seen as different names and forms of that Divine Power. This universe becomes our own body; the

different nations and its people become parts of our universal body. People who experience this are beyond any division. They become totally undivided and integrated personalities. Such personalities are the embodiments of pure, untainted Love. Expressing that Divine Love through all their words and deeds, they inspire people and transform their lives.

Together we are a power, an undefeatable power. When we work together, hand in hand, with love, it is not just one life force but the life energy of countless people, of the group, that flows in harmony, unimpeded. From that constant stream of unity, real progress will take place, and we will see the birth of peace.

A drop of water cannot be a river; a river is formed by numerous water drops. It is the joining together of countless drops that creates a flow. The real flow of life lies in unity, in the oneness that arises out of love.

Let us pray and meditate together. That is the way to reach the shore of peace. When we meditate and pray as a group, the life energy of all of us will harmoniously flow to a single stream spreading a divine fragrance soaked in

the sweetness of love. This will create vibrations of peace and unity in the atmosphere. Attuning our minds with the one Supreme Power and forgetting all thoughts of division, let us open our hearts and sincerely utter the following prayer:

LOKAH SAMASTAH SUKHINO BHAVANTU
Let all beings in all the worlds be happy.

During such moments of prayer, the vibrations of the prayer will reflect in the minds of everyone, thus giving peace and tranquillity.

Om shanti, shanti, shanti...
Peace, peace, peace...

Book Catalog
By Author

Sri Mata Amritanandamayi Devi
108 Quotes On Faith
108 Quotes On Love
Compassion, The Only Way To Peace: Paris Speech
Cultivating Strength And Vitality
Living In Harmony
May Peace And Happiness Prevail: Barcelona Speech
May Your Hearts Blossom: Chicago Speech
Practice Spiritual Values And Save The World: Delhi Speech
The Awakening Of Universal Motherhood: Geneva Speech
The Eternal Truth
The Infinite Potential Of Women: Jaipur Speech
Understanding And Collaboration Between Religions
Unity Is Peace: Interfaith Speech

Swami Amritaswarupananda Puri
Ammachi: A Biography
Awaken Children, Volumes 1-9
From Amma's Heart
Mother Of Sweet Bliss
The Color Of Rainbow

Swami Jnanamritananda Puri
Eternal Wisdom, Volumes 1-2

Swami Paramatmananda Puri
On The Road To Freedom Volumes 1-2
Talks, Volumes 1-6

Swami Purnamritananda Puri
Unforgettable Memories

Swami Ramakrishnananda Puri
Eye Of Wisdom
Racing Along The Razor's Edge
Secret Of Inner Peace
The Blessed Life
The Timeless Path
Ultimate Success

Swamini Krishnamrita Prana
Love Is The Answer
Sacred Journey
The Fragrance Of Pure Love
Torrential Love

M.A. Center Publications
1,000 Names Commentary
Archana Book (Large)
Archana Book (Small)
Being With Amma
Bhagavad Gita
Bhajanamritam, Volumes 1-6
Embracing The World
For My Children
Immortal Light
Lead Us To Purity
Lead Us To The Light
Man And Nature
My First Darshan
Puja: The Process Of Ritualistic Worship
Sri Lalitha Trishati Stotram

Amma's Websites

AMRITAPURI—Amma's Home Page
Teachings, Activities, Ashram Life, eServices, Yatra, Blogs and News
http://www.amritapuri.org

AMMA (Mata Amritanandamayi)
About Amma, Meeting Amma, Global Charities, Groups and Activities and Teachings
http://www.amma.org

EMBRACING THE WORLD®
Basic Needs, Emergencies, Environment, Research and News
http://www.embracingtheworld.org

AMRITA UNIVERSITY
About, Admissions, Campuses, Academics, Research, Global and News
http://www.amrita.edu

THE AMMA SHOP—Embracing the World® Books & Gifts Shop
Blog, Books, Complete Body, Home & Gifts, Jewelry, Music and Worship
http://www.theammashop.org

IAM—Integrated Amrita Meditation Technique®
Meditation Taught Free of Charge to the Public, Students, Prisoners and Military
http://www.amma.org/groups/north-america/projects/iam-meditation-classes

AMRITA PUJA
Types and Benefits of Pujas, Brahmasthanam Temple, Astrology Readings, Ordering Pujas
http://www.amritapuja.org

GREENFRIENDS
Growing Plants, Building Sustainable Environments, Education and Community Building
http://www.amma.org/groups/north-america/projects/green-friends

FACEBOOK
This is the Official Facebook Page to Connect with Amma
https://www.facebook.com/MataAmritanandamayi

DONATION PAGE
Please Help Support Amma's Charities Here:
http://www.amma.org/donations

www.ingramcontent.com/pod-product-compliance
Lightning Source LLC
Chambersburg PA
CBHW061345040426
42444CB00011B/3099